D0063939

In One Body through the Cross

THE PRINCETON PROPOSAL
FOR CHRISTIAN UNITY

———— ∞∞∞ ————

*A Call to the Churches from an
Ecumenical Study Group*

Sponsored by the Center for
Catholic and Evangelical Theology

Edited by

Carl E. Braaten *&* Robert W. Jenson

WILLIAM B. EERDMANS PUBLISHING COMPANY
GRAND RAPIDS, MICHIGAN / CAMBRIDGE, U.K.

© 2003 Wm. B. Eerdmans Publishing Co.
All rights reserved

Wm. B. Eerdmans Publishing Co.
255 Jefferson Ave. S.E., Grand Rapids, Michigan 49503 /
P.O. Box 163, Cambridge CB3 9PU U.K.

Printed in the United States of America

07 06 05 04 03   7 6 5 4 3 2 1

ISBN 0-8028-2298-3

www.eerdmans.com

IN ONE BODY
THROUGH THE CROSS

To the Churches of North America,
Judicatories, Ecumenical Agencies,
Ecumenical Officers, Laity and Clergy

Dear Colleagues:

The following document is the work of sixteen theologians and ecumenists, gathered from across the ecumene, who met for three years at Princeton, New Jersey, to consider what may be called the ecclesiology of ecumenism. In its form, the project was modeled on the *Groupe des Dombes,* founded in 1937, which pioneered many of the insights and formulations that enabled the successes of the post–Vatican II dialogues. The members of the *Groupe des Dombes* were not appointed by their Catholic, Reformed and Lutheran churches, and did not attempt to speak for them. Similarly the Princeton group was instituted and its members were chosen by an independent ecumenical foundation, the Center for Catholic and Evangelical Theology. The unofficial character of the Princeton Project provided members freedom to reflect creatively on the present situation and future possibilities of modern ecumenism. With this report, they do not claim to speak *for* their churches, but hope to speak *to* all the churches, out of shared concern for the founding ecumenical imperative "that they all may be one . . . so that the world may believe" (John 17:21).

The Center for Catholic and Evangelical Theology called the group together following consultations which showed wide consensus that both the ecumenical movement itself and the churches' commitment to it were stalled in place. "Reception" by the churches of consensus achieved in dialogues is even more difficult than expected. Some key points of division have proven unexpectedly stubborn. The institutions of conciliar ecumenism are largely captive to a "new ecumenical paradigm" which subordinates the concern of the "faith and order" movement, for the visible unity of Christians, to social and political agendas which are themselves divisive. The wisdom of the first general secretary of the World Council of Churches, Willem Visser 't Hooft, "The World Council of Churches is either a christocentric movement or it is nothing at all," now carries little weight. Perhaps most distressing, the churches that once principally carried the movement have turned their energies to other matters, often to their own internal divisions.

It is not that modern ecumenism has not achieved much, more than could once have been dreamt of. The bilateral dialogues have created a remarkable body of creative and ecumenically shared theology; particularly the "communion ecclesiology" is influential in many churches' thinking. *Baptism, Eucharist and Ministry,* produced by the Faith and Order Commission of the World Council, achieved unheard-of consensus by rooting itself in the apostolic tradition, and has been widely studied. The signing of the *Joint Declaration on the Doctrine of Justification* by the Roman Catholic Church and the Lutheran World Federation "consigned to oblivion" the mutual condemnations of the Reformation era. There have even been actual restorations of fellowship between separated churches. But the great divisions remain, and few see a way forward.

We will not in this preface further preempt the document. We say only that we fully approve the results to which the consultation has in fact come.

For the Center for Catholic and Evangelical Theology

CARL E. BRAATEN
Executive Director

ROBERT W. JENSON
Associate Director

In One Body through the Cross

THE PRINCETON PROPOSAL
FOR CHRISTIAN UNITY

1. For three years we have gathered from across the ecclesial spectrum for intensive discussions of the unity of the church. We together now propose, with the New Delhi assembly of the World Council of Churches (1961), that the unity which God promises and to which he calls his church is a unity of Christians "made visible as all in each place who are baptized into Jesus Christ . . . are brought by the Holy Spirit into one fully committed fellowship, holding the one apostolic faith, preaching the one Gospel, breaking the one bread. . . ." We propose that the churches' retreat from this vision is sin, which is visited upon the churches in their own internal weakness and unfaithfulness. We propose that the churches must now, both in sheer obedience and for their own healing, commit themselves anew to the biblical vision articulated at New Delhi. And we propose that there are steps — some described in our document but surely many more that others may discover — that can now be taken toward the unity promised and mandated by God. The way of obedience will require of our churches disciplines of self-sacrifice which we pray the Spirit may inspire, for we are redeemed only as the Spirit reconciles us "in one body through the cross" (Ephesians 2:16).

I. The Unity We Have and the Unity We Seek

2. In late modernity we fear unity, often with good reason. We cherish our particularity — our family and ethnic heritage, our established patterns of life and thought. We look with suspicion on the political and economic forces that impose homogeneity. We celebrate diversity and pluralism, sometimes as a good in its own right, because we fear the constraints of a single set of ideals.

3. Christians, however, proclaim unity as a gift of God. We understand our life of faith and discipleship as inseparably a call both to personal holiness and to participation in community. "There is one body and one Spirit," we read in the Epistle to the Ephesians, "just as you were called to the one hope of your calling, one Lord, one faith, one baptism, one God and Father of all, who is above all and through all and in all" (Ephesians 4:4-7). This Christian vocation to community has been realized not only in local gatherings, but in awareness of a deep, if less visible bond with the saints in other regions (2 Corinthians 8–9), with a family of communities throughout the known world or *oikoumene*.

4. Visible Christian unity is thus not a modern dream, but a permanent and central aspect of Christian life. It exists already, in virtue of our common faith which unites us in a single Savior; and it continues to call us beyond the differences of theology and worship that have developed over the centuries, to a deeper unity of common prayer, common witness, shared conviction, and mutual acceptance. Ecumenical concern arises from the perception that Christians belong together, and that the unity that is already ours must appear more fully in our worship, our mission, and the structures of our religious life. This sense of what Christian unity ought to be is rooted in the conviction that the unitive power of the Holy Spirit, however inadequately respected in the present life of the churches, is already real and effective.

5. Christian unity is given by God through the Holy Spirit. For that reason, our human efforts to deepen and perfect it are always rooted in prayer and in the proclamation of the word of the gospel, through which God acts to reconcile those who are estranged from him and from one another. "The mystery of [God's] will . . . , set forth in Christ as a plan for the fullness of time," Ephesians reminds us, is "to gather up all things in him, things in heaven and things on earth" (Ephe-

sians 1:9-10). The result of this unifying work of the Spirit is that peoples once hostile to God's chosen people "are no longer strangers and aliens, but . . . citizens with the saints and members of the household of God, built upon the foundation of the apostles and prophets, with Christ Jesus himself as the cornerstone. In him the whole structure is joined together and grows into a holy temple in the Lord" (Ephesians 2:19-21). Therefore the quest for a deeper unity among Christians is a discipline internal to the life of faith. It has two fundamental assumptions: (a) that Christian unity is an intrinsic part of the transformed life God works among those who live in the faith of Jesus, and (b) that it is a goal yet to be fully achieved in concrete, visible human terms.

6. (a) Because it is God who binds his people together in faith and love, work for Christian unity is always, in the end, an acknowledgement of God's present authority and activity. Ecumenism is not a concern for secular ideals of community, perhaps to be achieved at the expense of fidelity to normative tradition. In its origins and at its heart, ecumenism is a penitent awareness that our divisions contradict and jeopardize the gracious gift of God, who has already joined his children together as one body in the Spirit of his Son (Ephesians 4:3-4). The bond that joins Christians to God and to

14

each other, though grounded in the interior working of the Holy Spirit, is not meant to be invisible; it must have a visible edge. To work against the visible manifestation of the unity God has given us, or to accept its absence with resignation, is therefore resistance to God's Spirit and exposes us to God's judgment. St. Paul writes: "If anyone destroys God's temple, God will destroy that person . . ." (1 Corinthians 3:17). At the same time, God's grace, in this present history at least, is made visible only in human weakness. Of our churches as separated "bodies," as well as of each of us as disciples, we can only say with Paul that we are "struck down, but not destroyed . . ." (2 Corinthians 4:9).

7. (b) The gift of the church's unity remains, in Christ, a promise for the future. The fulfillment of this promise is a common life of shared worship, joint witness, agreed conviction, and mutual care, expressing the single vocation Scripture calls "the one hope of your calling" and rooted in "one Lord, one faith, one baptism" (Ephesians 4:4-5). By the word of the gospel, God assigns us to one another, in order that we may realize together the vocation of a common life and a common mission. The hope that this unity will come to perfection in faith and worship is integral to the Christian vo-

cation, and its present imperfection must not blind us to its necessity.

8. We can thus speak of two poles of Christian unity. On the one hand, a bond of faith and communion in Christ, established by the saving action of God, already exists among all disciples. On the other hand, God continues to summon and to draw us towards a deeper common life of reconciliation, mutual love, and shared labor, in which Jesus' prayer might be fully answered: "that they may become completely one, so that the world may know that you have sent me, and have loved them even as you have loved me" (John 17:23). The unity that already exists, founded on the apostolic faith, is the necessary presupposition of ecumenical striving on our part. The manifest imperfection of our unity, in worship and in the articulation of apostolic faith, reveals the goal and vocation of the whole Christian people.

9. From the gift and promise of unity grows a concrete challenge. If Christians are to realize the unity for which Jesus prayed, they need structures, institutions, and regular practices by which their communion in faith is expressed and formed — structures by which they are gathered together as one people of faith and

have access to one another for the sake of mutual care, joint mission, and common service to the world's needs. How this Christian communion is to be given structural form is the concern of ecumenical activity in the strict sense. Answers to it depend on theological convictions about the church itself as Christ's body, and about its mission: What does it mean for us to be one people in Christ? Under what conditions can it be said that our life and mission are genuinely shared? What forms of common worship, what instruments of Christian teaching, support, and mutual correction are indispensable to our life as Christians, if God is to bring his work of reconciliation and unity to fulfillment? Different Christian traditions will offer different answers. Roman Catholic and Orthodox Christians believe that specific features of historically legitimated authority and worship are necessary for communion in the faith and love of Christ. Many Protestant Evangelicals are convinced that structures of institutional unity must remain open to improvisation. Most "mainline" Protestants find themselves somewhere between these positions.

10. As theologians from churches across this spectrum, we do not offer a plan for the structural reform or institutional coordination of existing Christian bodies. We

simply insist that sustained attention to the structures and forms of communion, and to their foundation in a common faith and discipleship, is today a decisive aspect of our Christian vocation. Living in divided churches, Christians have become accustomed to division. We easily regard disunity as normal. But easy acceptance of Christian division is, we believe, as great a threat to the integrity of our churches as division itself. For where division is regarded as normal, is no longer perceived as scandal and wound, the gift of unity that is the "mystery of God's will," his "plan for the fullness of time" (Ephesians 1:9-10), will remain hidden by human ignorance and sin. To work towards the real and concrete growth of unity among all our churches is, we believe, an imperative for the conscience of every Christian.

II. A Brief History of the
Modern Ecumenical Movement

11. Concern to promote the structures and forms of Christian unity is not new. Within the modern period, the eighteenth-century revivals fostered, on Protestant ground, fellowship among believers of varied ecclesiastical allegiances, and joint commitment to propagate

1909 1908 - 120 German church Leaders gathered (Ecumenically) creat
[As a way of averting WWI] "Int'l Committee on friendship
as an attempt to create
goodwill. This Sponsor
Life Work Conf in Stockholm

the gospel over the face of the earth. In the nineteenth century, largely lay initiatives resulted in the formation of such organizations as the Evangelical Alliance and the Young Men's and Young Women's Christian Associations. The World Student Christian Federation acknowledged as its missionary goal both "that all may be one" and "the evangelization of the world in this generation." European and North American missionary societies, for the sake of concerted policy and practice, began a series of world missionary conferences; it is from the conference at Edinburgh in 1910 that the twentieth-century ecumenical movement is usually reckoned to date. After the First World War, the concerns of the Edinburgh Conference received institutional form through the foundation of the International Missionary Council.

12. While the ecumenical aims of these missionary movements were initially limited to practical arrangements for cooperation between existing Christian agencies, some participants saw a deeper connection between mission and unity. According to the prayer of Jesus, the unity of his disciples is an essential component in their witness to the world; disunity among them, in faith or in practice, is therefore a counter-testimony to the gospel. In line with this insight, the General Convention of the Protestant Episcopal Church in

for Missionaries

Issues were non-unification on dominant issues.
Also brought out New Divisions

the USA called in 1910 for a world conference on Faith and Order, a call that was taken up by members of other churches. Already in 1886 the bishops of this church had proposed as a universally acceptable basis for Christian unity what has come to be known as the "Chicago-Lambeth Quadrilateral": the canonical scriptures, the ancient creeds, the dominical sacraments of baptism and the Lord's Supper, and the historic episcopate "locally adapted in the methods of its administration." These four items came to be the main agenda of the Faith and Order movement through the twentieth century, beginning from its first world conference at Lausanne, Switzerland, in 1927. In 1920 the Orthodox Patriarchate of Constantinople sent an encyclical letter to "the churches of Christ everywhere," proposing a "fellowship of churches" that would foster rapprochement among them through study and cooperation.

13. Despite their common origins at the Edinburgh Conference, Faith and Order and the International Missionary Council did not always see eye to eye. Some in the Council were suspicious of the "ecclesiasticism" of Faith and Order; while Orthodox members of Faith and Order suspected Protestant mission activity of proselytism in Orthodox territories. Matters were further complicated by a third current in the stream of the

Note Per Dr. Plot: The Failure of Reformation in England was to produce a single National Protestant Church!

1) Roots are in Anglican Tradition *Orthodox were present in 1925 eStath + in 1927 eSwitzer

ecumenical movement, emphasizing the common social and political ideals of Christianity; a Universal Christian Conference on Life and Work met in Stockholm in 1925. This movement's activist slogan, "Doctrine divides, service unites," made for tense relations with Faith and Order (10% to Cath ix) *untrue!*

14. These three currents nevertheless contributed to the formation of a single ecumenical movement. The World Council of Churches was created by coalescence *merger* of the Faith and Order and Life and Work movements in 1948, and the International Missionary Council was integrated into the World Council in 1961.

15. The 1961 World Council assembly at New Delhi adopted what remains the most adequate and comprehensive description of "the unity we seek." This unity

> is being made visible as all in each place who are baptized into Jesus Christ and confess him as Lord and Savior are brought by the Holy Spirit into one fully-committed fellowship, holding the one apostolic faith, preaching the one Gospel, breaking the one bread, joining in common prayer, and having a corporate life reaching out in witness and service to all and who at the same time are united with the whole

Yves Congar – Ecumenical Theological leader in Catholic Diocese

Charles Brent – Came back to USA – (Missy in Philippines) he thought we need to help organize + World Conf on Faith on Order

Christian fellowship in all places and all ages, in such wise that ministry and members are accepted by all, and that all can act and speak together as occasion requires for the tasks to which God calls his people.

The New Delhi assembly recognized that "the achievement of unity will involve nothing less than a death and rebirth of many forms of church life as we have known them . . . nothing less costly can finally suffice."

16. Meanwhile, the Roman Catholic Church was about to enter the ecumenical movement officially. Pius XI had forbidden Catholic participation in ecumenical meetings for fear of "religious indifferentism," but some Catholics had engaged in a "spiritual ecumenism" of prayer for Christian unity "as and how Christ wills"; and the unofficial French *Groupe des Dombes* ventured into "theological ecumenism" as well. Transconfessional trends in biblical, patristic, liturgical, and other studies during the decade following the Second World War provided intellectual foundation for the surprising event of the Second Vatican Council (1962-1965). The Council's Decree on Ecumenism, *Unitatis Redintegratio*, following the establishment of the Secretariat for Promoting Christian Unity, made the Catholic Church a prominent participant in the modern ecumenical move-

ment. The Roman Catholic Church decided against membership in the World Council of Churches, but a Joint Working Group was formed. Roman Catholic theologians were appointed to the Faith and Order Commission, and played an important part in the elaboration of the "convergence document," *Baptism, Eucharist and Ministry* (1982), which became the most widely studied doctrinal statement of the modern movement. Roman Catholic ecumenism occasioned the development of the bilateral dialogues, which could treat divisive issues directly with a view to renewed fellowship. In his encyclical of 1995, *Ut Unum Sint,* John Paul II affirmed the Roman Catholic Church's "irrevocable" commitment to the ecumenical cause, which he described as the restoration of visible unity, in obedience to the will of the Lord, for the sake of a more credible witness to the gospel of reconciliation. The Pope recognized a certain "growth in communion" among all the Christian communities. He called for persistence in prayer, which he described as the "soul" of ecumenical renewal, and for dialogue centered on the "fundamental importance" of doctrine.

17. Already, however, there were contrary developments in the institutional circles of the World Council of Churches and in the governing bodies of many of its

member communities. A new general secretary of the World Council had before his election put forward, in 1989, the notion of a "paradigm shift" in the ecumenical movement. In his view the "christocentric universalism" of early twentieth-century ecumenism had rightly begun to give way to a broader theism that would give greater emphasis to God's more hidden work in the world. The ecumenical movement's earlier focus on "salvation history" was rightly being replaced by dedication to "care for the planet," and a corresponding emphasis on Life and Work concerns over those of Faith and Order and Mission and Evangelism. The ecumenical interest of many member churches also had begun to shift, from traditional Christian doctrinal and structural concerns to interreligious dialogue; while the membership of bilateral ecumenical bodies came more and more to be determined by gender and race rather than by theological qualification. That these tendencies were not universally accepted as healthy is shown by criticisms addressed to the World Council after its Canberra assembly in 1991. Orthodox participants observed an increasing distance between the Council and the constitutional basis articulating its original vision; Evangelicals objected to a lack of clarity about the relation between the revealed truths of revelation and contemporary concerns — legitimate enough in themselves —

24

in the areas of justice, peace and the integrity of creation. The Council attempted in the 1990s to formulate "a common understanding and vision," but few at the Harare assembly of 1998 thought this was accomplished. It is now generally agreed that the classical interests of Faith and Order and Mission and Evangelism have been marginalized in the Council.

18. The achievements of the twentieth-century ecumenical movement have nonetheless been great. It is vital that they be sustained and enhanced, until such time as God may grant their completion. The gospel has indeed been taken to every corner of the world. Separated churches have made genuine progress toward doctrinal agreement. From being divided in their prayers, Christian communities have discovered greater mutuality in worship of God, and have come to draw widely on the liturgical and devotional resources of each other's traditions. Churches have begun to consult together in matters that affect their common life; their ministers have begun to give pastoral care across institutional boundaries. In these and other ways, the "unity which is both God's will and his gift to his Church" is indeed "being made visible." But the process is far from complete, and grace left idle may be forfeit. We believe the New Delhi description of

unity remains the challenge for each new generation of ecumenists. It is our hope to remind the churches again, at the dawn of the twenty-first century, of the necessity and attraction of that vision.

III. Unity and Mission

19. A common life, in which those who were divided are reconciled in the body of Christ, is an essential goal of the mission that God has appointed for his people. Unity is not merely a means to mission, but rather a constituent goal: God gathers his people precisely in order to bring unity to a divided humanity. If we accept division from other Christians as normal and inevitable, we turn away from the mission God has given us.

20. Sin divides us against ourselves (Romans 7:15-22) and from one other. Therefore the gospel does not come into human communities only to address individuals in the privacy of the heart. The gospel is a public proclamation through which the Holy Spirit summons men and women from their locations within the human world to gather around a common center, the crucified and risen Jesus Christ. This movement takes concrete social form in the gathering of the Christian

assembly. In turn, the church becomes the corporate agent of the gospel's continuing proclamation of unity:

> But you are a chosen race, a royal priesthood, a holy nation, God's own people, in order that you may proclaim the mighty acts of him who called you out of darkness into his marvelous light (1 Peter 2:9).

21. The movement from our diverse social and ethnic locations to a new location in Christ is anticipated in the prophetic writings (Isaiah 2, 66; Joel 3; Zephaniah 3; Zechariah 8) and described and reflected upon throughout the New Testament. The New Testament paradigm is the reconciliation of Jew and Gentile in the end-time gathering of God's people. But God's gathering of those who have been divided extends further. Not only the divisions between Jew and Gentile but also those between male and female, slave and free, Greek and barbarian, rich and poor (Galatians 3:28; Colossians 3:11; James 2:1-5) are transcended by the new unity established in Christ.

22. It is easy to lose sight of this fundamental Christian truth. We may rightly celebrate diversity and difference. But diversity is easily conscripted to sinful purposes; and it is not easy to separate the diversity that

should be valued from the diversity that must be deplored. Cherished group identities, often rich in historical memories of nobility and courage, can be permeated with contempt for traditional inferiors, hatred for traditional oppressors, and fear of traditional foes.

23. The apostolic message does not affirm diversity for its own sake. It calls men and women of every human origin into a holy community and confers on them a new, shared identity in confession of the crucified and risen Lord. The life of the church thus calls for continuous critical sifting and reconstruction of human identity. Elements that constitute our differences must be questioned, judged, reconciled, and reconfigured within the unity of the body of Christ:

> But speaking the truth in love, we must grow up in every way into him who is the head, into Christ, from whom the whole body, joined and knit together by every ligament with which it is equipped, as each part is working properly, promotes the body's growth in building itself up in love (Ephesians 4:15-17).

The unity of the church does not therefore reduce difference to uniformity. In the New Testament the church is neither a zone of intimate sympathy among the like-minded nor a space of live-and-let-live. The unity of the church is rather the paschal unity of those who have been assigned to one another by a common Lord and summoned to a shared task.

24. The gospel gift and promise of unity exclude both divisive sectarianism and liberal indifference. The Christian affirmation of diversity is what the New Testament calls *agape,* urgent commitment to the good of the other, that regards even wrong done by the other as an occasion for communion.

> My friends, if anyone is detected in a transgression, you who have received the Spirit should restore such a one in a spirit of gentleness. Take care that you yourselves are not tempted. Bear one another's burdens, and in this way you will fulfill the law of Christ (Galatians 6:1-2).

Agape is more than sentiment or inward attitude. It is a common life into which we must enter.

25. If Christian unity should not be sentimentalized, neither should it be construed as a general principle of social harmony or communal cohesion. Christian unity

is neither human togetherness nor institutional self-preservation. It is a new life together, sanctified by the Holy Spirit, with apostolic form and content. Indeed, the New Testament supposes that one possible outcome of Christian unity is separation from the world. And when the teaching or behavior of other Christians is so captive to worldly powers that the gospel is falsified, true unity demands rejection of such behavior, not accommodation. We should, however, be careful about invoking such considerations to justify the present divisions among our churches. Many confessional and denominational families now contain within themselves far more serious divisions than those that once divided them from other Christian communities; this calls into question their claims that historic divisions are maintained solely for the sake of truth.

26. While the whole of the New Testament in one way or another assumes an inseparable connection between unity and mission, this is made explicit in two texts that have been especially important for the ecumenical enterprise.

27. The Epistle to the Ephesians presents the whole Christian mystery as the mystery of God's unification of all things in Christ (1:10), which takes form most concretely

in the reconciliation of Jew and Gentile "in one body through the cross" (2:16). This reconciliation, which already has taken place in the person of the crucified and risen Jesus (1:20-23; 2:4-7; 2:13-16), demands that we live in a way conformed to this reconciliation. Christian mission is the building-up of a new community in which those who were divided are now reconciled as a temple in which God may dwell on the earth (2:21-22). Ephesians thus sketches an amazing cosmic vision in which the very meaning and destiny of creation are displayed in the life of small Christian assemblies in which Jew and Gentile struggle to live together with Christ as their peace.

28. John 17:20-23 has in some ways been the charter-text of modern ecumenism:

> I ask not only on behalf of these, but also on behalf of those who will believe in me through their word, that they may all be one. As you, Father, are in me and I am in you, may they also be in us, so that the world may believe that you have sent me. The glory that you have given me I have given them, so that they may be one, as we are one, I in them and you in me, that they may become completely one, so that the world may know that you have sent me and have loved them even as you have loved me.

Three points must be made about this remarkable passage. First, the unity of which Jesus speaks must be in some way visible, because it is meant to be *seen* by the world. Invisible unity has no evangelistic power. Second, salvation, unity, and witness are intertwined. What binds together those who believe in Jesus is his gift to them of the glory he has himself received from the Father. To receive this gift is to be brought together with others into the unity of the church, and thus to become a sign to the world of the truth of Jesus' claim. Third, Jesus' prayer for the unity of the disciples must be read in the context of his commandment that they love one another (John 15:12ff.), which is explicitly grounded in the relationship of the Father and the Son (15:9). Jesus' prayer discloses both the mystery of grace by which alone the commandment can be kept and the communal context of shared life to which Jesus' prayer concretely refers.

29. If these texts are taken seriously, it becomes clear that the relationship between mission and unity is more than contingent and pragmatic. It is not only that our missionary efforts would be more effective were we to work together. Nor is it only that divisions among Christians discredit the message in unbelievers' eyes. Both are true, but neither captures the New Testament's way of linking mission and unity.

30. The New Testament is as clear about the dangers of division as it is about the imperative of unity. In 1 Corinthians 1, St. Paul denounces the divisions among the Corinthian Christians because they obscure the one Christ into whom all were baptized (1 Corinthians 1:13). By linking Christian division with issues of wisdom and power, Paul identifies the destructive dynamic of division. When Christians are divided among themselves, each group must distinguish itself from the others by claiming its own special "strengths" and "insights." Precisely so, they are committed to knowing something *other* than "Jesus Christ and him crucified" (1 Corinthians 2:2). Alongside the preaching of Christ there is inevitably now "boasting" (1:31) in the special virtues of the group, and the cross of Christ is "emptied of its power" (1:17).

31. St. Paul's warnings ring true for us. Much current preaching, catechesis, and discipline are emptied of the power of the cross of Christ. Nor are the "challenges of modernity" the only reason for the diminishment of Christianity in Western culture. The spiritual failure of Christianity in the modern era stems in many ways from ongoing division. Our complacency about division undermines our mission; we note three ways in which this happens.

32. First, the distinct identities of our churches tempt us to relish the special marks that distinguish our communities from others, and not to glory in the confession of the crucified Lord we share in common. In the past those special marks were often found in the doctrinal or disciplinary or liturgical traditions of confessional families. Today they are just as likely to be located in the special atmosphere or program of a local congregation. We are Roman Catholics or Lutherans or Methodists, or a "family-oriented" congregation or an "inclusive" or "traditional" congregation first, and Christians only second.

33. Second, our churchly identities lack the winnowing and transformative power of the gospel. Our missions in a particular place all too easily enter into complex collusions with divisions of class, culture, ethnicity, or status already present there. Rather than reconciling the divided, the gathering of men and women into churches may reinforce their divisions. In the United States this has been most evident in the case of the division between black and white, but it is also true with regard to other divisions, particularly those of class, which are less visible and more easily ignored. Churches thus become artifacts of specific cultures, and their mission becomes the reinforcing of folkways.

Even when churches break free from this role, their ability to impose corresponding discipline is compromised by the fact that anyone who is offended can simply walk down the street to another church. This is now increasingly true among clergy also, as they change loyalties according to shifts of spiritual priorities and denominational politics.

34. Third, present divisions corrupt even our best and most sincere commitments to unity. If we seek to intensify and extend loyalty to our traditions, in order to enhance international connections and ward off internal schismatic pressures, we risk emphasizing precisely those distinctive features — liturgical forms, confessional documents, practice of primacy, patterns of spiritual experience and traditions of exegesis — that divide us from others. Thus, we run the danger of enhancing denominational loyalty by "boasting" of something more unique than the gospel of Jesus Christ.

35. In all these three ways, division breeds never-ending diversion from authentic mission. Moreover, each such diversion tends to provoke reactions that are themselves equally destructive. Where mission has been conceived as the strengthening and expansion of one's

own Christian group, and this is seen to be wrong, there may be a concentration on social service that virtually silences evangelism of any sort. Where mission has been practiced as chaplaincy to some class or ethnic group, and this is seen to be wrong, a group may attempt to include the whole world within itself by sheep-stealing from existing churches. Where mission has been understood as therapeutic service to individuals, to the obscuring of the gospel's social implications, and this is seen to be wrong, the churches may strive for public presence through activism and advocacy, which if not accompanied by the building up of Christ's body as a distinctive people, only reinforce the churches' collusion with divisions in the society.

36. To point out these consequences of division is not to denigrate existing forms of Christian community. Nor does it necessarily contradict the high theological evaluation that some Christian communities give to structures and institutions to which they are committed. Nonetheless, the pervasive and debilitating consequences of division must not be ignored. No matter what our location in the scandal of Christian division is, no matter how we understand our responsibility for division, the burdens of disunity are shared by all. Therefore, no matter how we understand the roles,

structures, or status of our churches, denominations, and fellowships of faith, we must incorporate the imperative of unity into our mission. We must rejoice in the gift of unity that God gives. We must yearn for the fullness of reconciliation and mutual love promised in the return of our Lord. And most importantly, we must seek to discern the forms of communion that might draw us together in joint mission.

IV. The Division of Our Churches and Their Competence to Teach the Truth

37. The distortions brought on by division have consequences for the capacity of the churches to teach with authority and so to abide in the truth proclaimed by the apostles, for doctrinal decision-making and authoritative teaching are closely bound up with the apostolic mission. The church is charged to "hold firmly" (1 Corinthians 15:2) to the good news of Jesus Christ received from the apostles of the Lord, both in its own life and in its proclamation to the nations. But if a Christian community cannot agree on the apostolic legacy, its common life will be grounded and ordered on other bases and its corporate witness will be to something else. The distorted relation of the church's present-day

witness to the apostolic legacy therefore strikes at the heart of the church's existence. Normative teaching and authorized ways of ordering common life are necessary and essential elements of the church's apostolic existence.

38. Divisions among Christians distort and impair these central elements of community. Certainly this is true from a pragmatic perspective. There is abundant testimony from non-Christians to the confusion created by the witness of divided churches, all claiming to speak for the same Christ yet at odds with one another in their understanding of the truth and their practice of corporate life. In pluralistic liberal societies such as North America, the authority of church teaching is further undermined by the phenomenon of "church-shopping." The teaching of the divided churches and the ordering of their life are perceived not as assertions of life-giving, binding truth, but as selling-points for an array of consumer choices. Even tough-minded determination to resist cultural pressures can be viewed and indeed presented as another consumer option.

39. "Church-shopping" has resulted in movement in two directions. Some disaffected Christians move from churches in which norms of faith and life are more rig-

orously defined into other churches that are perceived as more congruent with the universal scope of God's love. Others, frustrated with more elastic communities, move into more stringently disciplined communities that are perceived as having greater integrity. Movement in either direction may be motivated by an honest concern for the gospel, but can also contribute to a covert redefinition of the norms of life and teaching within the community into which the convert moves. A norm may be valued not because it safeguards the church's apostolic legacy but rather because it affirms or rejects certain social and cultural trends.

40. This tendency to transform binding norms into consumer options is not simply the result of sociological forces. It reflects a deeper spiritual malaise, which developed especially in the wake of the splintering of Western Christianity in the sixteenth century. In every separated community the temptation has been to base the community's life on its "distinctives," that is, on the features of its faith and life that differentiate it from other Christian communities. The apostolic faith confessed in the ecumenical creeds, intended to differentiate the church from truly spurious "Christian" communities, is pushed to the margin of communal self-description.

41. The differences between divided churches were originally understood as fundamental disagreements about the content and significance of the apostolic legacy. Dispute therefore took the form of argumentative exegesis of Holy Scripture, in which the great Christian teachers and witnesses of the past were called to give testimony. But as the dynamic of division unfolded, actual dispute between separated Christians became less common, and when it did occur often served as a kind of ritual revalidation of division. Theological teaching in separated churches more and more took the form of a monological presentation of the distinctive doctrines and practices of a particular community. The relationship of theological teaching to Scripture and the tradition of Christian witness became less direct, with Scripture and tradition serving less as the text that theology expounds and more as the body of evidence to which theology appeals to validate the strengths of a particular community. In the nineteenth and twentieth centuries, it became common for confessional theology to appeal to the phenomenology of a community's form of life and teaching, to the ethos discerned in the community's distinctive history. There was a profound shift in the way that norms of life and teaching were perceived: the question "Is it true?", that is, faithful to the divine revelation, was implicitly equated with "Is it au-

thentically Catholic?", "Is it Evangelical?", "Does it express the mind of Orthodoxy?", "Is it congruent with the dynamics of the Reformation?"

42. This shift from truth to identity reflects a kind of tribalization of Christian communities, an implicit redefinition of the separated churches as quasi-ethnic groups, each with its unique history and outlook, its distinctive traditions, mores, and folkways. In some settings this tribalization has played into the hands of secular nationalism and compromised the church's role amidst ethnic conflict. But in North America it more often has played into the hands of the consumerist dynamics of modern liberal society, in which identity is ever shifting. In this situation, some Christian groups have adopted a strategy of cultural accommodation. Others have more resisted the cultural fluidity of modern society, but often more for the sake of identity than for the sake of truth. In these circumstances, even the most sincere efforts to establish and enforce norms of faithfulness to the apostolic message lose credibility. The very fact of division insinuates doubt as to whether such norms are really based on discernment of the one gospel or arise rather from institutional or cultural self-maintenance.

43. The instability and confusion which Christian division introduces into normative teaching and the ordering of practice in our churches can be overcome only if we commit ourselves to the cause of visible unity. To be sure, Christian churches have always displayed some variety in their formulation of teaching and the organization of their life, and doubtless will continue to do so. Nevertheless, the authority of normative teaching and practice will continue to be undermined in all the churches until they present to the world a far more visible consensus in essential teaching and practice, based upon common reception of the apostolic legacy and its gospel truth. However loudly our rhetoric insists that Christian discipleship is not a matter of consumer choice, the point will be made effectively only when potential believers encounter all around them Christian communities united in shared disciplines of faithfulness to the apostolic word.

V. Accepting the Ecumenical Challenge

44. Congregational and parish life in the United States often proceeds with little sense of contradiction between division from others and life as a realization of the one church of Christ. This unawareness is indeed

related to positive developments: greater tolerance and the willingness of many individual Christians to accept members of other churches as brothers and sisters in Christ. But friendly division is still division. We must not let our present division be seen as normal, as the natural expression of a Christian marketplace with churches representing different options for a variety of spiritual tastes. Consumerist values and an ideology of diversity can anesthetize us to the wound of division. Recovering from this ecumenical anesthesia is one of the strongest present challenges to faithfulness.

45. Members of the Princeton Project come from various churches and have varying convictions about the shape that full, visible unity should take. We have differing judgments about the role of ordained ministry, the place of the sacraments, the role of bishops and of the bishop of Rome. We agree, however, that the unity we seek must be unambiguously visible, "so that the world may believe" (John 17:21). Unity must be recognizable as unity without an extensive theological gloss. One must be able to see that the church, in its ordinary life and practice, is one community reconciled in Christ.

46. Therefore we believe that the New Delhi statement (see §15) continues to state the ecumenical goal to which

we are called. Judgments about the precise form of the unity of "all in each place" depend on theological conviction and assessment of the current situation; and past patterns of unity, even those of the New Testament, cannot simply be taken over. But the New Delhi statement propounds three fundamental elements of unity that are particularly relevant to our time: (a) unity of faith and doctrine ("holding the one apostolic faith, preaching the one Gospel"), (b) a coordinated life of witness and service ("having a corporate life reaching out in witness and service to all"), and (c) reciprocity of membership and ministry in continuity with the church throughout the centuries ("united with the whole Christian fellowship in all places and all ages, in such wise that ministry and members are accepted by all"). These three aspects of unity defined by the New Delhi statement guide us toward concrete action.

47. (a) Authentic commitment to unity is always commitment to unity in the truth of *faith and doctrine*. When truth and unity are played against one another, both are misrepresented. In many American churches, doctrinal discipline is collapsing and internal divisions are emerging. In these circumstances, effort is often focused on the maintenance of present denominations' mere institutional unity, without reestablishing unity

of apostolic faith and doctrine. In order to defend doctrinal discipline, renewal movements in some churches justifiably threaten bureaucratic forms of unity, but this resistance is often itself local or denominational. Modernist and revisionist distortions within Christianity are best addressed by a united Christian voice under a common doctrinal discipline.

48. Renewing doctrinal discipline requires developing forms of common teaching and witness to the apostolic faith across a wide spectrum of churches. This is not an unrealistic dream. To a great extent, *Baptism, Eucharist and Ministry* has functioned as common teaching. Many Protestants who struggle to maintain a faithful Christian voice find encouragement in the Roman Catholic magisterium and the Orthodox tradition. The scholarship of the liturgical movement of the twentieth century was integral to the development of an ecumenical consensus on the centrality of the eucharist in the church's life. Many free-church congregations formally and informally respect common teaching authorities.

49. To build upon these successes, *we urge the following steps:* First, churches should routinely include theologians from other traditions in doctrinal commissions

and consultations. Second, official statements by churches should always be formulated for the widest possible Christian audience. Third, educational institutions that serve denominations should hire and encourage scholars who will teach in ways that serve the whole church.

50. (b) Greater coordination of *witness and service* was one of the founding impulses of the ecumenical movement, and it continues to mark an important area of ecumenical success. The joint political action of pro-life Evangelicals with Roman Catholics on the moral issue of abortion has done more to break down old habits of hostility than any theological discussion. Furthermore, the increasing secularity of Western societies is making re-evangelization a common Christian project that transcends historical divisions and theological differences.

51. There are negative trends as well as positive ones. Mutual witness and service can disintegrate into mere ideological commonality rather than genuine Christian cooperation. This happens when practical judgments about how best to serve the common good become the defining feature of common work. Thus judgments about third-world debt or the inviolability of private

property can take on near-doctrinal status. In such cases, secular principles and expertise supersede Christian principles of discernment as the basis for cooperation. This has come to characterize many initiatives of the National Council of Churches and the World Council of Churches. The result is a party mentality founded in political ideology rather than unity grounded in the Christian imperative of justice and charity.

52. In this context, *we urge the following steps.* Opportunities for coordinated witness and service should be affirmed and expanded. Missionary strategies should be developed across denominational lines, so that church growth is not accomplished by sheep-stealing but rather by evangelization of the unbaptized and re-evangelization of the lapsed. Protestant missionaries to historically Roman Catholic and Orthodox societies must be able to articulate the ways in which their work builds up the *whole church* in those places. Joint social and political action must be continually consecrated in common prayer.

53. (c) A possessive attitude toward *membership and ministry* often prevents ecumenical agreements from achieving concrete reality in local churches. Clergy

may welcome agreements establishing full communion, but at a practical level resist reciprocity of membership. Until leaders of local churches see their members as baptized into the whole people of God, there will be no visible unity of all in each place.

54. Our group does not agree about the theological meaning of ordained ministry. We do agree with the New Delhi statement, and affirm that recognition and reciprocity of Christian leadership are necessary elements of the visible unity we seek. Thus theological differences sometimes prevent reciprocity of ministry, but institutional forces make reciprocity unlikely even in the case of theological agreement. Trained to serve their churches, the clergy are socialized into the particulars that have divided them. Their professional advancement is defined by denominational structures that are threatened by significant advances toward Christian unity. Unity is a professional liability even when it is a spiritual commitment. Church leadership is as difficult to share as is membership.

55. Against the present lack of reciprocity of membership and ministry, *we urge the following steps.* We envision two very different situations: where agreements of full communion are in place, and where full com-

munion does not exist. In the first instance, church leaders in each place should work to implement existing agreements. In order to promote common mission, lay members should be encouraged to worship and serve in congregations in partner denominations. Among ordained clergy, churches should identify a ministry of unity, and seminary training should intentionally prepare ministers to serve in partner churches. In the second instance, where theological agreement is only partial and no authorized reciprocity of membership and ministry exists, congregations of separated Christians should pray for one another. When baptism is mutually recognized, this should be plain in the manner of its administration. The ecumenical vocation of married couples from separated communions should be acknowledged and supported by the churches. When full communion does not exist, churches should acknowledge and encourage special vocations for the sake of unity. God may call lay and ordained members of one church to sustained participation in the life and mission of separated churches, even if sacramental communion is not possible for a time. Such vocations do not deny real theological differences or disrespect canonical order but rather are a call to endure separation as a discipline which sharpens passion for unity. Such sacrifice is perhaps possible only for a few, and it will certainly take many forms, often partial and hidden. The churches should seek to identify and champion these vocations as a gift of the Holy Spirit to the divided churches.

56. The New Delhi statement provides vital guidance for the future; our suggestions by no means exhaust the possibilities. We believe that these suggestions are realistic, not in the worldly sense of relying on human motives, but in the godly sense of relying upon the cross of Christ. For in the cross of Christ, the personal and corporate suffering entailed in giving up aspects of our denominational heritages becomes the grace of fellowship with the Son, who brings us to the Father in the power of the Spirit. Unless and until Christians risk new forms of ecumenical endeavor, along the lines suggested, division will continue to undermine the clarity and cogency of Christian witness.

VI. Our Ecumenical Responsibilities

57. As the wound of disunity affects all Christians, so all churches and Christians are called to be agents of unity. This burden does not, however, fall on all in the same way. The possible agents of unity range from individu-

als to worldwide conciliar bodies. No one agent is suffi-
cient. Each must do that which is within its compe-
tence.

58. Individuals and groups of Christians who lack official standing have greater freedom for new initiatives.
The group producing this statement is an example of
such an unofficial gathering. Precisely because we do
not function in this group as official representatives of
our churches, we can speak more freely. It is our conviction that those unconstrained by bureaucratic roles
and free from the limitations of official leadership have
a distinctive call to the service of unity.

59. Local churches, both in the form of congregations
and parishes and in the regional form of dioceses, pres-
byteries, etc., have their decisive ecumenical role to
play. So long as local churches do not see themselves as
agents of unity, division will not be seen as a matter that
touches them. The congregation down the street must
be a matter of concern, not only on special occasions
or in a purely formal way, but as an element in the regular ordering of the internal life of the local church. Local churches should find structured ways to be respon-
sible to one another in mission.

60. Denominational structures and congregational associations play a central ecumenical role. These agents have achieved important advances in bilateral discussion and action. Nonetheless, denominational structures and congregational associations manifest a will-to-survival that consistently limits ecumenical action. Pension funds, endowments, and clergy rosters are so denominationalized that even profound theological agreements fail to overcome these institutional embodiments of division. We are convinced that the official leadership of American churches can play a full role in ecumenism only if this denominational mentality is overcome.

61. In the past, the National Council of Churches of Christ in the U.S.A. and the World Council of Churches have been important ecumenical agents. In recent years, they have become increasingly irrelevant to the pursuit of unity, as political and social agendas have pushed aside concern for unity in the confession of the faith and in the sacraments (see §17). Faith and Order concerns do not define the full extent of ecumenism, but they are essential elements of any ecumenism worthy of the name. If these councils are to regain their ecumenical importance, they must recover the quest for

visible unity, defined by the New Delhi statement, as their reason for being.

62. The worldwide organizations of the Protestant churches, for example the World Methodist Council or the Lutheran World Federation, were formed to deepen and extend their own traditions. They have a complex ecumenical role. They have performed valuable services of unity. They have increased the accountability of North American Christians to their denominational brothers and sisters throughout the world. They have supported important ecumenical dialogues with other worldwide bodies, especially with the Roman Catholic Church. Nevertheless, while such deepening and extending of one's own tradition can be carried out in service of the whole church, when it becomes an end in itself, it is an obstacle to unity. These bodies must see themselves as agents of unity among those who share their common tradition, but also on behalf of the wider church. They must recognize their provisional status.

63. The theological commitments of Roman Catholics, Orthodox, and to a lesser extent Anglicans prevent them from regarding their episcopal structures of worldwide governance as provisional. However, those

committed to the sacramental importance of their church structures must distinguish between the divinely appointed functions of oversight and ministry, and current juridical, bureaucratic, and institutionalized forms of those functions. To the extent that these current forms have been shaped by Christian division, they should be regarded as provisional and subject to change.

64. No churches are untouched by Christian disunity, but not all are touched in the same way. The self-understanding of the churches in relation to division is quite different. We cannot provide a definitive account of this diversity. However, it is our conviction that some churches and Christian movements have special responsibilities in our time.

65. In the present situation, the Roman Catholic Church has a special ecumenical place and must play a unique role. Including approximately half the Christians in the world, it is an essential agent in any comprehensive realization of church unity. While the papacy is undoubtedly a continuing stumbling block for many, the bishop of Rome is also the only historically plausible candidate to exercise an effective worldwide ministry of unity. This privileged role creates a great

burden of responsibility. The bishop of Rome and the magisterium of the Roman Catholic Church must teach in a fashion capable of shaping the minds of the faithful beyond those currently in communion with Rome.

66. We see three ways in which ecumenical commitment should shape Roman Catholic magisterial teaching. First, the Roman Catholic Church should resist the temptation to return to pre–Vatican II forms of theology, which were profoundly influenced by anti-Protestant polemics. Second, the bishop of Rome should recognize the special responsibility for unity implied in the claim to primacy and universal pastoral jurisdiction and should discharge the papal office in the spirit of sacrificial service to separated sisters and brothers in Christ. Third, the magisterial deliberations of the Roman Catholic Church should regularly involve non–Roman Catholic consultants. If the bishop of Rome is to teach for and to all the baptized, he must receive reliable counsel regarding the faith and life of the entire Christian community.

67. Evangelical and Pentecostal Christians and their institutions also have a unique role. All churches may benefit from their vitality, their zeal for evangelism,

and their commitment to Scripture. They demonstrate a spirit of cooperation with each other and sometimes with others that breaks down old barriers, creates fellowship among formally estranged Christians, and anticipates further unity. The free-church ecclesiologies of some Evangelicals bring a distinct vision of unity to the ecumenical task.

68. We see four ways in which Evangelicals could both benefit from and contribute to ecumenical commitment. Rather than being absent from formal ecumenical discussions, they should accept invitations to participate. Rather than presuming others' faithlessness and spiritual death, they should discern and celebrate living faith beyond their boundaries. Rather than acting out of an isolationist and sectarian spirit, they should practice hospitality and pursue catholicity. Rather than teaching a truncated vision of the apostolic tradition, they should recognize the historical legitimacy, charismatic authority, and spiritual vitality of other forms of Christian language and practice. Finally, rather than employing their resources solely to benefit their own fellowship or to call fellow Christians out of their fellowships, they should work for the health of all Christian communities.

69. Within the ecumenical movement, the Orthodox churches have insisted that the One Church is indivisible and that the perpetuation of denominationalism contradicts the norm of unity. This witness has been vital to the beginning and authenticity of modern ecumenism. Orthodox continuity with the ancient tradition has reminded all churches of their common origins. Orthodox liturgy and spirituality have reinvigorated prayer among Christians and shaped it to the ancient heritage, both of which contribute to unity. Yet, regretfully, the Orthodox churches have clung also to divisive and nationalistic proclivities. These should be abandoned. If that were done, the Orthodox witness would be enhanced, to the great benefit of all Christians.

VII. One Body through the Cross

70. We all suffer from the wounds of division. These wounds extend into our theologies, our institutional structures, and our very sense of what makes the church life-giving. Significant aspects of our traditions must be rethought if they are truly to witness to the one apostolic faith rather than to our divisions. Therefore we must examine our collective consciences and

repent of actions, habits, and sentiments that glory in division.

71. The disciplines of unity are penitential. As St. Paul teaches, for the sake of unity we must be willing to suspend gospel freedom and conform to the limitations of the weak. This process will be ascetical; it will necessarily involve the sacrifice of real but limited goods for the sake of greater good. We are convinced, however, that this ascetical dimension is necessary if the ecumenical project of modern Christianity is to move forward. Unity will require our churches not only to renounce the selfishness and insularity that we all dislike and easily see as sinful. It will also require our churches to embrace a spiritual poverty that has the courage to forego genuine riches of a tradition for the sake of a more comprehensive unity in the truth of the gospel.

72. We have no illusions about the prospects for success. Short of a decisive intervention of the Holy Spirit, the full visible unity of "all in each place" described in the New Delhi statement does not lie in the immediate future. However, the call to serve the unity of the church is not premised on the likelihood of success; that is in God's hands. Our present unity, however broken by our habits and traditions of division, already ex-

"Give up limited good for the sake of a greater good."

ists as a gift of God, and thus the unity we seek will not be simply a human work. This is good news, for we can trust the promises of the gospel. We propose the disciplines of unity as central to the Christian vocation, however filled with the pain of renunciation and sacrifice, however partial and provisional in worldly consequence they may be. Any true steps toward unity will be a manifestation of new life in Christ, as he reconciles us in one body through the cross.

Christian World Commuin (CWC)
 —Lutheran World Federation
 — World Alliance
 — World methodist Corp.

Members of the Study Group
and Signatories of the Princeton Proposal

*(institutional affiliation is given
for purposes of identification only)*

WILLIAM ABRAHAM, Perkins School of Theology,
Dallas, Texas

MARK ACHTEMEIER, Dubuque Theological Seminary,
Dubuque, Iowa

BRIAN DALEY, University of Notre Dame, Notre
Dame, Indiana

JOHN H. ERICKSON, St. Vladimir's Orthodox
Theological Seminary, Crestwood, New York

VIGEN GUROIAN, Loyola College, Baltimore,
Maryland

GEORGE LINDBECK, Yale Divinity School (emeritus),
New Haven, Connecticut

Lois Malcolm, Luther Seminary, St. Paul, Minnesota

Bruce McCormack, Princeton Theological Seminary, Princeton, New Jersey

R. R. Reno, Creighton University, Omaha, Nebraska

Michael Root, Trinity Lutheran Seminary, Columbus, Ohio

William G. Rusch, Faith and Order Foundation, New York, New York

Geoffrey Wainwright, Duke Divinity School, Durham, North Carolina

Susan K. Wood, St. John's University, Collegeville, Minnesota

Telford Work, Azusa Pacific University, Azusa, California

J. Robert Wright, General Theological Seminary, New York, New York

David Yeago, Lutheran Theological Southern Seminary, Columbia, South Carolina